Make Your Own Sock Puppets!

Tips & Techniques for Fabulous Fun!

Text and Puppets Created by

Diana Schoenbrun

Photographed by F. William Lagaret

Mud Puddle Books
NEW YORK

Make Your Own Sock Puppets! Tips & Techniques for Fabulous Fun
Text and puppets created by Diana Schoenbrun.
Photography by F. William Lagaret.

© 2006 by Mud Puddle Books, Inc.

Mud Puddle Books, Inc.
54 W. 21st Street
Suite 601
New York, NY 10010
info@mudpuddlebooks.com

ISBN: 1-59412-160-5

Designed by Michelle Gengaro

Printed and bound in China

Contents

Sock Puppet Creations

Ever have dreams of being a puppeteer? Sock puppets are a great way to start. Everyone can enjoy
them and the fun is infectious. Sock puppets are so easy
to make because they are made from materials that are
found around the house. Just give free reign to your
imagination and you'll soon be making animals,
people, monsters and other creatures.

Creating a sock puppet is just
the start of the fun. You'll find
that sock puppets can be used
in a variety of mirthful ways.

For example, making up sto-
ries is particularly exciting when
you have 3-dimensional characters
that can play the roles. Both children
and adults can use their puppets for story-
telling. Try reading from a book or play, and act out the
scenes with the puppets. Make a whole cast of different
sock puppet characters and then invite your friends and
family to put on a puppet show.

Or throw a sock puppet party and have everyone bring a sock and extra materials to share. Write down different characters on separate pieces of paper. Put the paper in a hat and have everyone pick a character to create.

Sock puppets can be used to make learning more fun. Use sock puppets to help learn the alphabet or counting. Why not use a puppet to practice singing a song? Communicating new ideas with the puppets is easy because puppetry is exciting and holds everyone's attention.

Making sock puppets allows you to be creative and nothing makes a better gift than something you create. Give a friend a sock puppet that looks like their favorite pet or make one that looks just like them!

Socks, socks, and more socks

There are so many types of socks to choose from when designing a sock puppet. Best of all, you can use socks with holes or socks that no longer fit. Recycling in this way is certainly better than throwing away. Collect unwanted socks from friends and family. Use a sock that has lost its match. Turn a sock inside out if you want a fuzzy texture. Most importantly, always remember to wash your socks before making your puppet. Look in your sock drawer and you may find that you already have a treasure trove of unwanted socks, all of which would be great for making sock puppets.

Look for socks such as these:

- stretchy socks
- cotton crew socks
- tube socks
- athletic gym socks
- toe socks
- novelty socks
- knee high socks
- trouser socks
- ankle socks
- wool socks
- striped socks
- patterned socks
- slouchy socks
- pom pom socks

Getting started

Here are some of things you might use to make spectacular sock puppets. Most of these materials can be found at home or at art and craft stores.

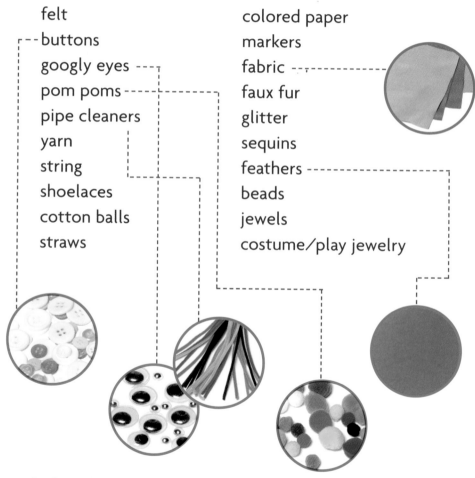

felt
buttons
googly eyes
pom poms
pipe cleaners
yarn
string
shoelaces
cotton balls
straws

colored paper
markers
fabric
faux fur
glitter
sequins
feathers
beads
jewels
costume/play jewelry

Other helpful tools

Craft glue is good for attaching materials to your sock. It makes a stronger bond than a basic school glue or glue stick.

Needle and thread may be used as well for attaching pieces. Always ask an adult for help when sewing.

Scissors for cutting. Be careful using scissors and have an adult help.

Making your sock puppet

Eyes can be made using buttons, felt, googly eyes, and pom poms. You can also draw eyes using a fabric marker.

Noses can be made from buttons, pom poms, and felt. The nose can be as detailed as you like.

Make nostrils by pinching the sock together in the center

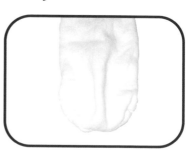

and add a few stitches to secure.

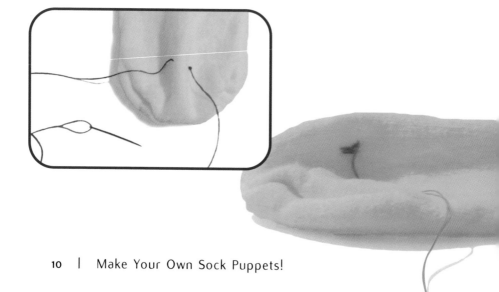

Next pinch the sock
fabric forward on each
side to create two nostrils.
Sew a few stitches on
the left and right side
to secure.

Then cut a piece of felt shaped like the letter 'm'.

Glue or sew each side underneath the centerpiece.

Now cover the nostrils with the felt snout.

Use glue or sew to secure.

Mouths can be formed a few ways.

The easiest way to create a mouth would be to use the natural fold of the sock.

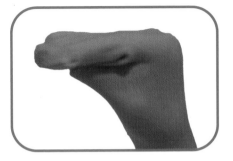

It's easy to add detail to the mouth by gluing or sewing a felt tongue in the sock fold.

For an even more detailed mouth, glue or sew a dark colored fabric oval on the sock and place a felt tongue in the center of the oval. Finally, felt teeth can be added around the mouth.

Ears can be made from felt, fabric, and paper.

Cut different shapes for ears depending on your character. Attach ears with craft glue or stitch them onto the sock with a needle and thread.

Hair can be made from yarn, string, or ribbon.

For yarn hair cut a 5 to 7 inch (12.7 to 17.8 cm) strand. Loop the yarn and knot at one end.

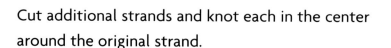

Cut additional strands and knot each in the center around the original strand.

You're creating a sock toupee!

Use glue to attach
to the sock.

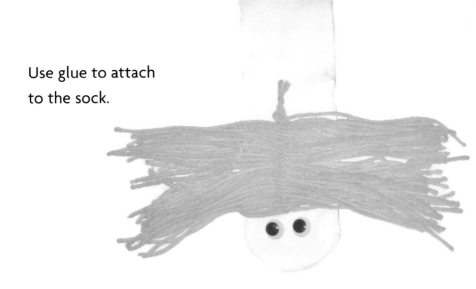

Felt can also be cut to create a mane of hair. Faux fur
is fun to use too.

Tails can be made many different ways. Pom poms and cotton balls are perfect for shorter tails. Long tails can be made from ribbon, yarn, string, shoelaces, and felt.

You can cut a single strand of felt for a simple tail.

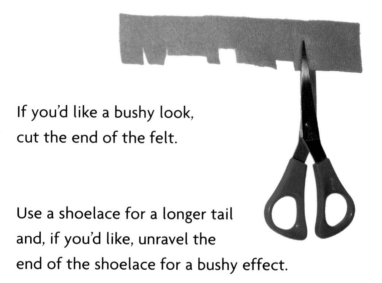

If you'd like a bushy look, cut the end of the felt.

Use a shoelace for a longer tail and, if you'd like, unravel the end of the shoelace for a bushy effect.

A more complicated tail can be made with a pipe cleaner and felt. Bend the pipe cleaner in half and twist. Leave a small loop at one end.

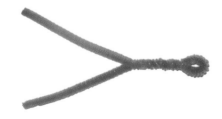

Cut the end of a felt strand to fray and wrap it around the pipe cleaner.

Then secure the felt with craft glue or sew a few
stitches to hold.

Sew through the
pipe cleaner loop and
attach the tail to the sock.

Whiskers are easily made with pipe cleaners.

Three small pipe cleaners can be used.

Twist two pieces at the center twice to form an X.

Then take the third pipe cleaner and twist around the center of the first two pipe cleaners.

Sew the whiskers to the sock at the center of the pipe cleaners before adding a nose.

Antenna can also be made with pipe cleaners.

The easiest way is to fold
a pipe cleaner in half
and bend any way you wish.

To make the antenna sturdier and flexible,
twist two pipe cleaners together.

Bend the pipe cleaners in half at the center
and flatten slightly.

Sewing pom poms on the ends
makes an interesting effect.

Finally attach the antennae
to the sock by adding
a few stitches where the
pipe cleaner is bent.

Accessories can make your puppet more unique.
Add glitter and gems to make your sock puppets
sparkle. Jewelry and beads are good materials to
dress them up.

Photo Gallery

Breathtaking Birds

penguin

flamingo

dodo

parrot

Out-of-this-World Aliens

little
green
alien

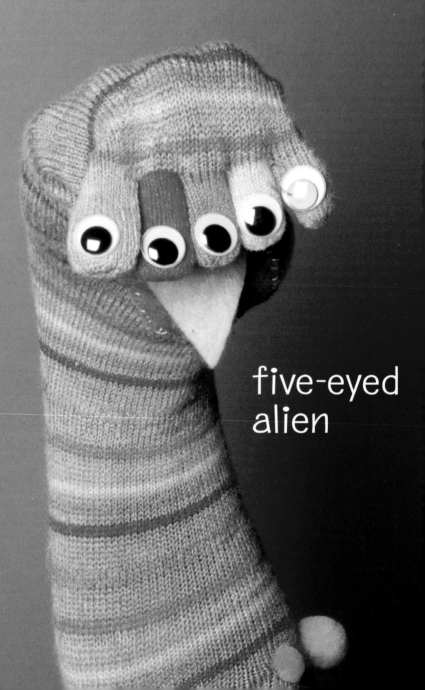

five-eyed
alien

Farmyard Friends

horse

sheep

pig

In the Garden

weed

flower

Creepy Crawlers

bee

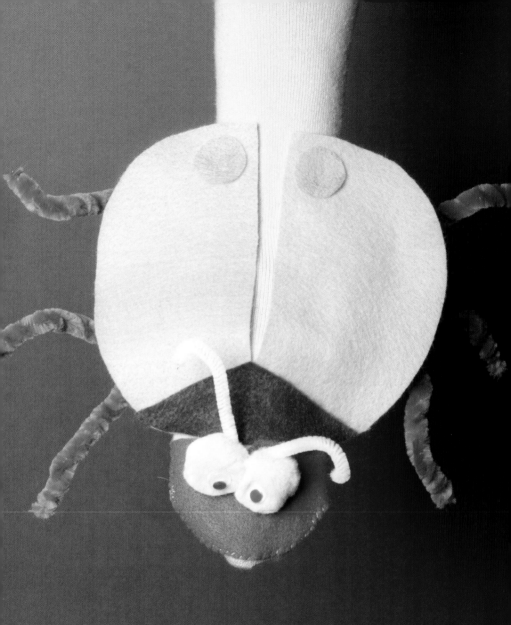

beetle

spider

butterfly

ladybug

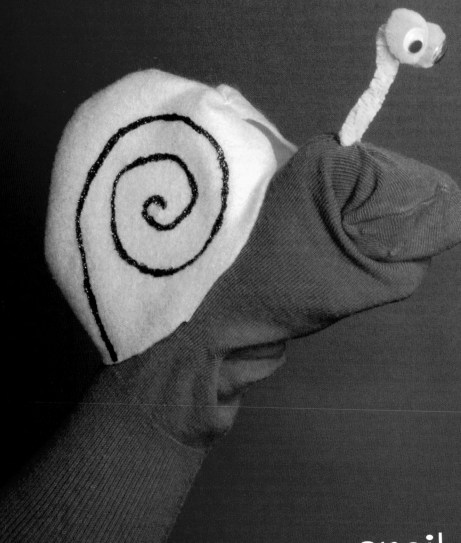

snail

Little Red Riding Hood

big bad wolf

Little Red

Snakes
Lizards
and
Turtles

snake

turtle

striped
snake

alligator

Furry Friends

reindeer

skunk

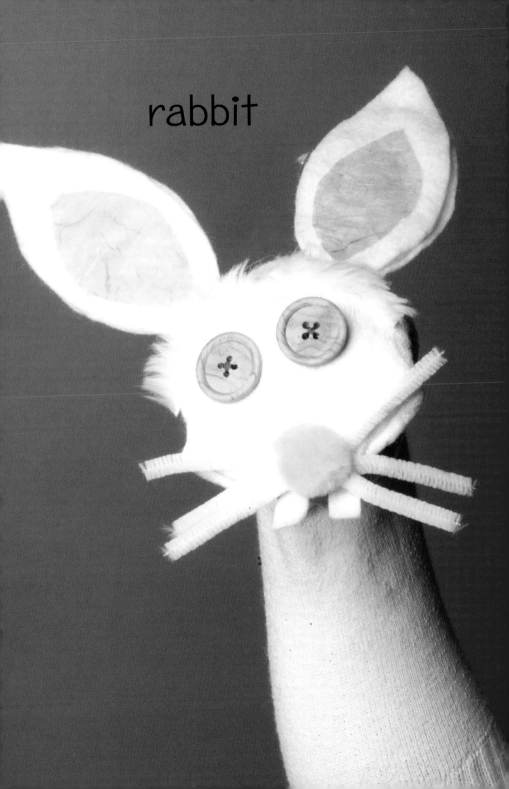

rabbit

The Argyle Family

papa

mama

spot

Dogs
Cats

and
Mice

dog

cat

mouse

Rapunzel

Royal Roll Call

prince

princess

Under the Sea
the Sea

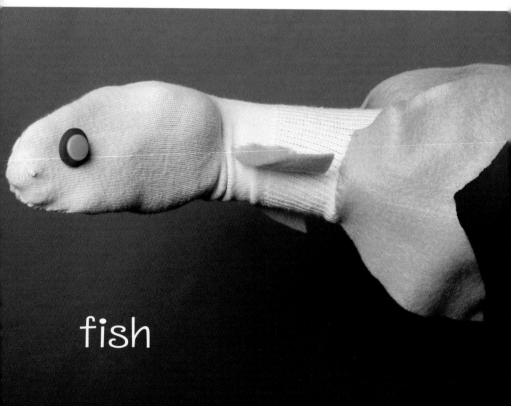

fish

octopus

Superheroes

Wild
Animals

elephant

hyena

giraffe

zebra

lion